The Brooklands Miniature Railway

"The Brooklands Miniature Railway"
is an original idea by the author Graham Lelliott.
It contains a detailed study of the miniature railway at
Brooklands Pleasure Park in Worthing, West Sussex,
from its conception in 1964 right up to the present day.

Graham Lelliott

GW00655870

201005963

The Brooklands Miniature Railway

10 Digit ISBN 0-9553893-2-1
13 Digit ISBN 978-0-9553893-2-0

Published by;
Graham Lelliott, 3 Busticle Lane, Sompting,
Lancing, West Sussex, BN15 0DH, England
Website: www.grahamlelliott.co.uk

Printed and bound in 2008 by;
CPI Antony Rowe, 48-50 Birch Close,
Eastbourne, East Sussex, BN23 6PE, England
Tel: + 44 (0)1323 434700
Website: www.antonyrowe.co.uk

Contents

Introduction

Having already written two other books, "A German Bomber on Worthing Soil" and "The Field Place Mystery", I wanted another local subject to be able to research and write about.

After much thought and consideration I decided to write about the miniature railway at Brooklands Pleasure Park, situated 1.5 miles east of Worthing town centre. The reason for this choice is that I have always lived approximately 1 mile away from the park and that the railway holds many childhood memories for me and for many others I am sure.

Brooklands Pleasure Park is owned by Worthing Borough Council and is a popular attraction all year round. Along with the railway, it boasts a large lake, motor boats, pedalos, a paddling pool, children's play areas, a pitch and putt course and a go-carting circuit. It also offers many large grass areas to play games or enjoy a family picnic and has a café to be able to enjoy its refreshments. All of the attractions and the café are however privately owned.

Before the park, part of the site was a rubbish dump. The dump became the pitch and putt course and the storm water reservoir at the end of the Teville Stream became the boating lake. There was landscaping and together the two components of the former wasteland gained popularity as a place where the family could relax and have fun.

It has become quite a challenge researching the subject, as the railway has always been privately owned. Despite this I feel I have covered all there is to know about the miniature railway and hope that the reader finds it of some interest, which may also trigger childhood memories for them.

All photographs, plans and other sources used have been acknowledged and copyright permission granted. However if something has been overlooked then this is down to human error and is completely unintentional.

Graham Lelliott

The History of the Railway

It all began in 1964 when a Mr David Stanier and a Mr Ernest Woods proposed a railway for the site. The Worthing Herald dated 11th September 1964 and titled "Brooklands mini-trains" wrote about this proposal and explained; "Brooklands open space at East Worthing may have its own miniature railway when the summer season opens next year.

The idea is that of the present licensees of the boating lake, Mr D. Stanier and Mr E. Woods, who have bought a £2,000 layout including an 11ft scale working model of an American Yankee Clipper engine complete with cowcatcher, bell and tender. The engine will be fired with Welsh steam coal and will haul six or seven coaches carrying up to 50 children at about four-mph.

The scheme has already been considered by the Parade and Open Spaces Committee, which has now asked for a detailed report from its officers. The report is to go to a special meeting of the committee next Thursday, when it is expected a decision will be taken and a recommendation made for the next Town Council meeting.

"This engine and tender is pretty well a collectors piece," Mr Stanier, a former engineer and loco enthusiast told the Herald. "It is in fact a very unusual type of loco, perfect in every detail. It has been looked after by experts – first class steam engineers – and we shall be doing the same for it when we get it. We were fortunate in knowing the previous owner and we got the first offer.

It comes from Danson Park, Bexleyheath, and is the one on which I used to ride with my daughter when she was a child. The track is 9½-inch gauge and the engine stands at just over 2 ft high. We plan to put the track along the western side of the boating lake from near the car park at the northern end, running along side the pitch and putt course to the southern end, where the lake overflows the weir into a culvert to the sea.

It will be a single track with a loop line for uncoupling the engine so that it can turn round for the return journey. We also expect to have small station layouts at each end of the track, with perhaps halts alongside the run." The Herald continued to say; "Mr Stanier, who hopes to have the layout ready by next Easter, emphasised that the loco was a quiet, clean running engine with practically no smoke.

Mr Woods, who originally suggested the railway for Brooklands, and Mr Stanier regard the railway as another attraction for the area, supplementing their boating and sailing facilities and those of the children's playground provided by the corporation nearby. "Unfortunately Brooklands is not as well known as it should be. We have never liked fairground rowdyism and we have always catered for family trade," said Mr Stanier. "We think this railway will increase our family amusement facilities here."

What the newspaper article does not say is that the miniature railway at Danson Park, Bexleyheath had closed and the owner, Mr Ron. C. Hammett, was about to immigrate to Bermuda due to ill health. Ron Hammett sold one of the locomotives, a 4-6-2 engine called "Princess", along with some spare track and coaches to a Mr Alan Bloom at Bressingham, Norfolk, and the remaining stock was sold to Mr Stanier and Mr Woods.

This photograph appeared in the Worthing Herald on 18th September 1964. The text below the photograph read; "A working model of an American Yankee Clipper engine that may be operating on Brooklands open space next year if plans to set up a miniature railway mature." (Worthing Herald and Gazette / Portsmouth Publishing and Printing Ltd)

Ron was originally reluctant to sell his collection to Stanier and Woods as neither had experience in steam locomotives and he was very concerned that they would not look after the collection in a professional way. In the end Stanier and Woods convinced him that Worthing Borough Council's engineering team had offered to help keep the locomotives maintained, although no evidence of this has been proved.

The "£2,000" collection was finally sold to them, which included a steam engine called "Lake Shore", a new petrol locomotive, several coaches and about 2,000 feet of track, including 5 points. "Lake Shore" was built by a Mr W. L. Jennings in 1934 as an American style 4-4-2 tender loco and two years later was sold to a Mr V. Burgoyne. Ron Hammett acquired this loco in 1942.

The photograph above shows the steam engine "Lake Shore" in Danson Park on the day in 1964 that the miniature railway was sold. The people in the background are Ron Hammett, the two purchasers Woods and Stanier and Ruth Hammett, which I understand, is Ron's niece. This was the last time anything was steamed as by that evening a lot of the track had been lifted and the Danson Park Railway was no more. (Derek Smith)

The eight-wheeled petrol mechanical locomotive, which was also sold to Stanier and Woods as part of the collection, was built by Ron Hammett in 1964. It is not clear how this locomotive was powered, however it was either a 6 ½ hp Velos Graveley or a 6 ½ hp Merry Tiller engine which I understand would have come from a rotivator or a similar agriculture machine.

A plan for the proposed miniature railway was drawn in September 1964 by a Mr J. Wilkinson, the Borough Engineer Surveyor and Planning Officer for Worthing Borough Council.

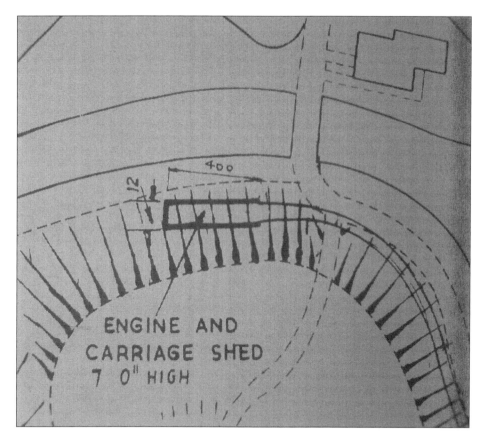

The north section of this plan is shown above. One can see the proposed engine and carriage shed, the footbridge over the Teville Stream and the public conveniences. Although no station platforms were planned, the north station would be located at the bottom right of this image.
(Worthing Borough Council)

Due to the size of the Borough Engineers plan, it was not possible to reproduce it for this publication. However the proposed railway was drawn in to run along side the west bank of the lake, then terminating at the weir at the south end of the park. The terminus is seen below, with the A259 Brighton coast road shown at the bottom right of the image. (Worthing Borough Council)

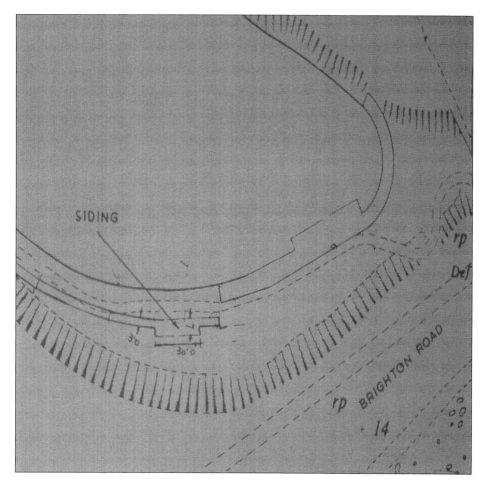

The proposed miniature railway plan also noted that a "typical section through track foundation" would contain a 1½-inch depth of ¾ inch graded aggregate between the track and sleepers and a further 3-inch deep "consolidation" of 1½-inch graded aggregate. It was also noted that the track would be 9½-inch gauge and that the total width of the track bed would be 3ft.

The Worthing Borough Council minutes for the meeting held on the 17th September 1964 stated that; "The Committee have to report that Messrs. Woods and Stanier, boat operators at Brooklands, have requested permission to operate a miniature railway along the west bank of the Brooklands lake.

They have pointed out, in support of their request, that a miniature railway would increase the popularity of Brooklands and that the Corporations café and pitch and putt course would benefit by increased receipts. A drawing showing the route and proposed buildings was submitted by the Borough Engineer.

Messrs. Woods and Stanier have intimated that in view of their financial commitments in connection with the purchase of the miniature railway and the erection of a shed to house the rolling stock, they would like the Corporation to bear the cost of the preparation of the ground for the railway track, estimated by the Borough Engineer at not exceeding £500.

The rent payable could take into consideration the fact that this amount of money has been expanded by the Corporation. A licence for seven years would be required, on the basis of a peppercorn acknowledgement for the first 12 months, and payments of £130 per annum for the remaining six years.

Messrs. Woods and Stanier indicated, in addition, that they would like to link the boating rights with the right to operate the miniature railway as this arrangement would be more economical in regard to the employment of labour.

The boating rights expire in March, 1966, and the operators ask that these rights be terminated at the end of March next and that a grant for seven years be given to them from 1st April next at a rent of £200 a year, which amount is due and payable by them during the year 1965/66.

RESOLVED, that subject to approval of the Finance and Law committee to the expenditure on the preparation of the ground for the railway track, and that (i) the necessary foundation work for the miniature railway be undertaken by the Council; and (ii) the existing licence in connection with the operation of boats at Brooklands be cancelled with effect from the end of March, 1965, and that from the 1st April next Messrs. Woods and Stanier be granted seven year licences in respect of the miniature railway and the boating rights on the above mentioned terms and such other conditions as the Town Clerk considers are necessary to be incorporated in the licences. (Note – The Finance and Law Committee have approved the additional cost.)"

In October 1965 an "artists impression" of the proposed engine and carriage shed was drawn by Mr J. Wilkinson, the Borough Engineer surveyor and Planning Officer for Worthing Borough Council. The "artists impression" can be seen below. Note the Teville Stream footbridge and the path which leads to the paddling pools, which incidentally were built in various animal shapes. (Worthing Borough Council)

The proposal for a railway at Brooklands had finally been accepted, however work to build the railway did not begin until early 1965. Not only would ballast and track have to be laid but also many small cuttings would have to be dug and re grassed.

The proposed engine and carriage shed was also constructed, measuring 40ft in length, 12ft in width and 7ft in height. This concrete building was in fact a standard car garage, similar to a Marley garage and was purchased in kit form from Sompting Concrete Products, in Rectory Road, Sompting.

This mammoth task was achieved on schedule and the 660-yard "end to end" railway, with "run round loops" at either end, was officially opened in time for the Easter period in 1965.

The photograph seen above appeared in the Worthing Herald,
dated 23rd April 1965. The caption below the photograph read;
"The latest attraction at Brooklands, a miniature railway along the west
bank of the boating lake, pleased hundreds of Easter visitors of all ages."
(Worthing Herald and Gazette / Portsmouth Publishing and Printing Ltd)

A close up of "Lake Shore" is seen below. I would imagine the steam locomotive is about to reverse to couple up with the coaches in the station. Note the lamp at the front of the loco, which I understand was added by Ernie Woods and David Stanier. Note also the old Southdown double decker bus in the background, travelling along Western Road. (Nick Kelly)

"Lake shore" departs the north station on what appears
to be a very quiet day at the park. (Nick Kelly)

"Lake Shore" heads back to the north station with the
pitch and putt course on the right. (Nick Kelly)

The "run round loop" and station at the south end of the line.
(Nick Kelly)

A rare photograph of the eight-wheeled petrol mechanical locomotive can be seen below at the south station. I would assume that the loco has just been uncoupled from the passenger coaches and will "run round", and re-couple for the return journey. As one can see, the driver was positioned in a separate four-wheeled coach, attached to the drive unit. The loco was blue and yellow in colour and named "007", presumably after Ian Fleming's fictional British Secret Service character, James Bond. Many of the houses in the background would not stand for much longer as flats would later be built on the site.
(Nick Kelly)

"Lake Shore" is seen below in action, having just left the station. Driver Frank Geal is seen in the driving seat. Note two of the children on the train are grabbing blades of grass from the bank, a third even appears to have a rounders bat hanging out the carriage! (Des Weller and Linda Niall)

The railway had proved to be very popular. As a result of its popularity, minutes for a Worthing Borough Council meeting, held on 17th September 1965, stated that; "The Town Clerk submitted a letter, dated 16th August, from Messrs. E. Woods and D. Stanier, operators of the miniature railway, asking for permission to lay additional track, as shown on the drawing now submitted.

Track is now laid along the west side of the boating lake and the proposal includes the laying of track round the remaining part of the lake, including the building of a bridge in close proximity to the existing bridge at the north end of the boating lake.

RESOLVED, that permission be given on the condition that the work, including detailed design, is carried out by Messrs. Woods and Stanier to the satisfaction of the Borough Engineer and that no cost devolves upon the Corporation."

"Lake Shore" sits quietly outside the shed, without the tender. The chalk board on the front of the loco states; "Please do not touch anything on this loco."
(Nick Kelly)

In this view, "Lake Shore" is seen sitting opposite the north boat office.
Houses along Western Road can be seen in the background.
(Des Weller and Linder Niall)

Almost a year had passed and still no changes had been made to the railway.
On the 16th September 1966, the miniature railway was again mentioned in a
Worthing Borough Council meeting.

The minutes stated; "The Town Clerk submitted a letter from Messrs. Woods
and Stanier stating that they would like to extend the miniature railway round
the lake and in this connection asking whether the Corporation would be
prepared to construct a bridge at the north end of the lake and prepare the land
on the east side of the lake for the laying of the track, on the understanding that
the Corporation would be reimbursed the cost, as agreed, over a period of
years.

Messrs. Woods and Stanier are proposing to purchase track with a wider gauge
and new rolling stock and they state that if they cannot proceed now with the
extension they will have to spend about £500 on track points to commence the
return journey which expenditure will be abortive if at some future date the
arrangements are made for track to encircle the lake.

The Borough Engineer reported that at present no technical time is available for the preparation of drawings in connection with this suggested extension and that the Corporation labour is not available to carry out the work. He estimated the cost of the work involved at £1,200.

RESOLVED, that the Finance and Law Committee be informed that this Committee favour an extension of the track as suggested and that they be asked whether they would agree in principle to the Corporation bearing the cost of the proposed works to be repaid over a period of years terminating at the same time as the existing licence in 1972 on the understanding that Messrs. Woods and Stanier will arrange for the preparation of drawings and also the engagement of a contractor to carry out the works.

(Note – The Finance and Law Committee have agreed in principle to the proposal that the Corporation should bear the cost of the proposed works to be repaid over a period of years, subject to the Borough Engineer being satisfied with the design and manner in which Messrs. Woods and Stanier intend to carry them out.)"

The railway was also discussed in a meeting on 11th November 1966. The minutes stated that; "With reference to paragraph 3 on pages 258/59 of the printed minutes, the Borough Engineer reported that in connection with the extension of the miniature railway around the lake he was now satisfied with the design of the proposed works and the manner in which Messrs. Woods and Stanier intended to carry them out. The Town Clerk reported that Messrs. Woods and Stanier had requested that they be granted a licence for seven years instead of five years to operate the railway over the additional area. This would necessitate an extension by two years of the period of operation of the existing agreement.

RESOLVED, that Messrs. Woods and Stanier be granted a 7 year licence, commencing in 1967, to operate the miniature railway at Brooklands, subject to the terms of an agreement to be prepared by the Town Clerk and to payment by Messrs. Woods and Stanier of the following acknowledgements: - (a) in respect of the extension of the track now proposed - £230 per annum (exclusive) for 7 years; and (b) in respect of the track covered by the existing agreement dated 31st December, 1964, to the continued payment of £130 per annum (exclusive) for the years 1967, 1968, 1969, 1970, and 1971; and for the remaining two years, the acknowledgement to be such as shall be negotiated later."

Plans were finally drawn up for the proposed extension by Worthing Borough Councils Borough Engineer Surveyor and Planning Officer, Mr J. Wilkinson. Once again due to the size of this plan, I have been unable to reproduce it for this publication. However part of the plan is seen below and shows the current south terminus, marked with the letter A. The extension can be seen passing the weir, travelling over the footpath and continuing along the eastern bank of the lake. (Worthing Borough Council)

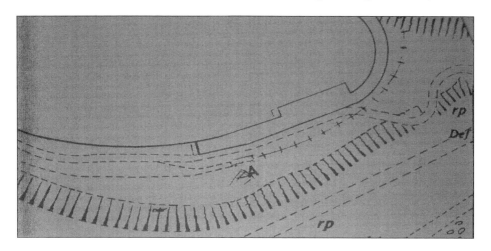

The image below shows the north end of the plan where the new railway bridge would be built to take the railway over the Teville Stream, where it would then form a complete circuit, as shown here by the letter B.
(Worthing Borough Council)

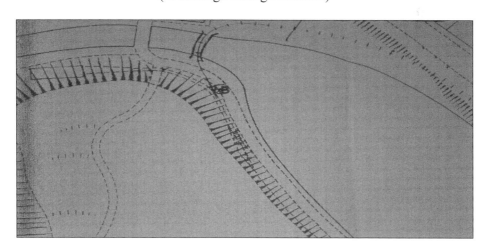

The photograph below shows "Lake Shore" heading south. Although the steam loco retained its original name when it was brought to Worthing, it seems as though the engine was often referred to as "The Brooklands Belle." Note the boating landing stage on the right of the photograph and lack of trees and foliage, which is now a familiar sight at the park today. (Doris Walker)

Now the proposals had been accepted, work was able to begin. The existing 9½-inch gauge track was taken up and the two locomotives and carriages were no longer needed. The petrol loco, "007", was sold to the Lakeland Railway at Severn Beach, Gloucestershire and now survives in private ownership in Berkshire. It is interesting to note that throughout its history it had been re-gauged to 10 ¼, 7 ¼ and then back to 9 ½. The steam engine, "Lake Shore", was sold to Cherry's, a dealer in Richmond, Surrey and is now owned by a gentleman in Essex. Sadly it is not clear what happened to the track and carriages, although it is possible that Cherry's also had this.

A brand new collection, which included, a British Railways blue, class 52 Western locomotive called "Western Comet", six accompanying BR blue "toast rack" style carriages and just over 1,760 yards of 10¼-inch gauge track was purchased from the miniature railway builder Severn Lamb Ltd in Stratford upon Avon. The track was delivered to the park in January 1967, although the locomotive and carriages would remain at Severn lamb Ltd until the track had been completely laid. It is not clear whether this was Wood's and Stanier's wishes or whether it was a recommendation from Severn Lamb Ltd.

"Western Comet" was the first of only four of their class to be built by Severn Lamb Ltd. It also happened to feature on the front cover of the 7th July 1967 edition of Model Engineer Magazine and was shown sitting outside Severn Lamb's workshops. This front cover of this magazine can be seen below. (Model Engineer Magazine / Encanta Media)

each month
Volume 133   Number 3324

Model Engineer

MAP HOBBY MAGAZINE

WESTERN COMET

Model Land-Rover ● 5 in. gauge tank locomotive

The "Cover Picture" text shown on the following page explained; "A fine 10 ¼ inch gauge diesel locomotive built by Severn Lamb Ltd of Stratford-on-Avon, in collaboration with David Curwen, for Woods and Stanier, Brooklands Park, Worthing. It is powered by a Ford Anglia engine, is about 15 foot in length and weighs approximately one ton."

The ground for the track extension on the east bank was prepared. This involved digging many new cuttings to keep the railway on the level. One of these banks had an 80-foot long retained wall built to keep the bank in place. Several tons of ballast was ordered and sparingly laid along the route. The new 10-¼ inch gauge track was then laid along the original track bed, past the original terminus at the weir, along the east bank and over the newly constructed Teville Stream railway bridge, where the track would join the start of the journey, thus forming a complete circuit. The original station location and white fence was retained, but still no platforms were built.

A point was added to the north side of the station, which took an additional line alongside the Teville Stream to the existing engine and carriage shed. Before entering this shed, two points were added making the track split into three. These tracks were embedded in concrete, giving them that "tramway" look. Concrete was also used to build four crossings along the route. Now the track had been laid, Stanier and Woods advised Severn Lamb Ltd to deliver the locomotive "Western Comet" and the six accompanying carriages. These were delivered to the park on Saturday 18th March 1967.

The brand new stock is seen above at the station with Ernie Woods standing on the right. David Stanier can be seen in the center and appears to be taking a closer look at the locomotive. (Des Weller and Linder Niall)

"Western Comet" is seen here passing over the new railway bridge. The newly built café can be seen on the left. (Nick Kelly)

The new railway featured on the front page of the Worthing Gazette on Wednesday 22nd March 1967. A photograph of "Western Comet" leaving the Teville Stream railway bridge was also shown. Sadly the quality of the photograph was exceptionally poor to reproduce and so it has been omitted.

The newspaper explained; "This gleaming blue and white miniature diesel engine has attracted crowds of youngsters to Brooklands Park since it arrived on Saturday. It is a unique handmade scale model of a Western Enterprise engine and is called the Western Comet. With a top speed of 20 miles an hour it can pull six carriages with about 70 passengers."

The Worthing Gazette continued to explain; "Throughout the winter Mr David Stanier and Mr Ernest Woods, who operate the railway, have been laying more track and have built a bridge across the lake. The track now completely encircles the lake and is a mile long. The Western Comet cost £1,600 and about £5,000 has been spent on improving the railway this winter."

"Western Comet" is seen above with the shelter in the background.
This shelter was for some reason often referred to as "the bandstand".
(Des Weller and Linda Niall)

The locomotive had been supplied with two brass "Western Comet" name plates and two builders work plates which read; "Design by David Curwen – Made by Severn Lamb Ltd – 1967 – Stratford on Avon." One of these builders work plates could also be found at one end of each carriage. Woods and Stanier wanted each carriage numbered (1-6) and BMR (Brooklands Miniature Railway) lettering added to the sides of the carriages, however at the time, Severn Lamb Ltd did not offer this option.

It is not clear where the numbers and lettering were cut, although it is possible a local engineering firm made them. Woods and Stanier may have even cut them although this is unlikely, as the pair would have been engrossed in track laying. The letters W and S (Woods and Stanier) were also made up and would have been drawn on the steel sheeting, one overlapping the other, then cut out as one piece. Several of these and the BMR lettering were made. Cut from ¼ inch thick sheets of steel, the numbers and lettering were riveted to the sides of the carriages and then painted yellow.

The photograph above, taken shortly after the 10-¼ gauge line had opened, shows "Western Comet" passing over the crossing by the boat landing stage. Note the missing roof panel on "Western Comet", which was often omitted to give more ventilation to the engine on hot days. Concrete repairs made to the path, due to the insertion of the new track can also be seen. (Lesley Stanier)

In this view, the class 52 Western loco has passed over the Teville Stream bridge and is about to enter the station. The track to the left leads to the engine and carriage shed. By now tarmac had replaced the lose ballast at the station and a new white picket fence had also been erected. (Lesley Stanier)

By the time this photograph had been taken in 1967, a grill had been inserted into the yellow front of the locomotive, presumably to give the engine more ventilation. (Trevor Rowe)

Now the lakeside railway was well established, Woods and Stanier looked forward to developing the railway even more. In September 1967 planning permission was requested to build a 120 foot tunnel. Minutes for a Worthing Borough Council meeting held on 15th September 1967 stated the following;

"The Borough Engineer submitted request from Messrs. Woods and Stanier, the operators of the miniature railway at Brooklands, to construct a tunnel 120ft long with an appropriate length of track at their own expense on land on the eastern side of Brooklands lake in substitution for the existing track at this point. RESOLVED, that the request be granted subject to the work being carried out to the satisfaction of the Borough Engineer and to the terms of a licence to be prepared by the Town Clerk."

Anyone expecting to see brick built portals at each end with a mound carefully landscaped into the existing area would be deeply saddened, as for some reason, this project never came to fruition. However many have explained that they recall passing through a temporary tunnel made out of arched corrugated steel, similar to that of an Anderson air raid shelter. If this was the case, the tunnel would have been short lived.

An old postcard can be seen above. It was available in and around Worthing during the late 1960's and early 1970's. (Constance Postcards Ltd)

It soon became evident that a purpose built station would be needed. Stanier and Woods visualised two concrete platforms with a wooden shelter, which would run the entire length of the west platform. This shelter would incorporate a ticket office and a waiting room, and would be built using cedar wood with asbestos sheeting for the roof. The application and plans were submitted to Worthing Borough Council on the 11th October 1967.

Two days later the station proposal was discussed at a Worthing Borough Council meeting. Minutes for the meeting explained; "The Borough Engineer submitted an application from Messrs. Woods and Stanier to construct a small railway station to the north east of the lake in accordance with the drawings now submitted. RESOLVED, that subject to planning approval being obtained, the proposal be approved."

On 1st November the Town Panning Department explained; "The location of this station would appear to be reasonable but I am rather concerned about the length – 75'0" and the materials – particularly the corrugated asbestos roof. The structure adjoins the mound so the roof is going to be especially visible and should be felt covered I think – possibly green. To Borough Architect for comments please."

The Borough Architect replied to the Towns Planning comments sent on 1st November and explained; "I agree with the Towns Planning comment. Far too long. Green felt roof. I would query also the following: 1) Due to its open form the cross bracing will show, which in this case will look unpleasant. Covered with fibreboard? 2) Ticket and parcel office would look better joined together at the south end. Both window apertures should be rectangular. 3) Lettering blue. Facia black or white. Return to Town Planning - 8/11/67."

Woods and Stanier had become concerned about the comments made and felt obliged to write a letter to Worthing Borough Council. Their letter, dated 5th December 1967 explained; "We feel it is necessary to produce this letter with the drawings of the proposed station, in order to make quite clear, the reasons for certain aspects of the design.

Firstly, we urgently need the station, and it must be functional. We need it because at present we are unable to run effectively due to being unable to control the people who board the train at all sorts of places in the temporary station at present in use. This leads to a certain amount of unpleasantness among the passengers and we don't like that.

Obviously the platform must be long enough to accommodate the train and of equal height with the coach floors each side of the track. These are essentials for safety. Reference the general design, we are trying to make it match the café building nearby, i.e. natural cedar boards, flat roof, white facia boards and as short as possible waiting area so as not to make the structure too long. At the same time it must be long enough, or it's no use. It requires an office each end, partly for use and partly for rigidity of design. These we have made long as possible, consistent with appearance and usefulness. One is naturally a ticket office and the others a parcel office, etc.

It may not be generally appreciated that quite a number of our customers come from long distances and have several pieces of baggage etc and we are always asked to look after it for them. Now we must mention the most important thing of all – shelter from the constant southwest wind, which is, and always will be a big problem at Brooklands. We lose many, many customers through this and so we must of course, have a back to our station. People just won't stand around in the wind waiting for a train ride, and will appreciate a covered seating area, still being able to view the boats, etc.

This is the ideal layout for a miniature railway station, developed after 3 years of deserving the special points connected with the business and after taking advice from leading experts in the field. In short then, we wish to expect a small station, pleasing in appearance – functional in design – and with a view to generally tiding up the railway, and at some time making a small contribution towards solving a most pressing problem – shelter for the people who sometime come from many miles away to enjoy the family amenities at Brooklands Pleasure Park. We trust that our proposal will be accepted and that we may proceed as soon as possible in order to avoid the worst weather, and make a good clean job of it."

A revised plan was reissued, where fortunately all parties concerned were able to accept the new changes. This plan was approved with conditions on 8th December 1967 and Stanier and Woods were finally able to continue with the project and make the revised plan a reality.

Sompting Concrete Products were used once again, although on this occasion would provide the wood for the station building. Ex employee Chris Taylor recalls; "The company had a wood shop, used to make the moulds for the concrete products. I was given the measurements to cut the wood to size." Once completed the 'kit' was then past on to David Stanier and Ernie Woods.

Titled "Brooklands Miniature Railway proposed station", the plan included a front, end and top view of the station. The front elevation is seen below and shows the overall length of the building, not including the roof, measuring 59.9 ft. Despite the Councils concerns about the length of the original station, the platform length measures 98 ft including the ramps at each end. (Worthing Borough Council)

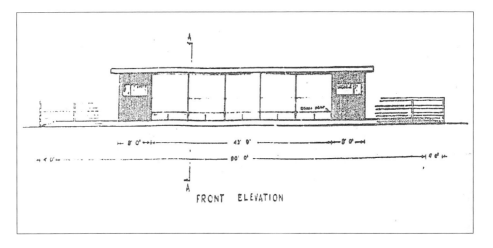

FRONT ELEVATION

The top view is seen below and shows part of the roof removed to see the roof supports, bench seat and luggage office detail. The west platform, which accommodates the station building, measures 8ft wide, whereas the east platform measures only 2ft 6 inches. The gap between both platforms also measures 2ft 6 inches. (Worthing Borough Council)

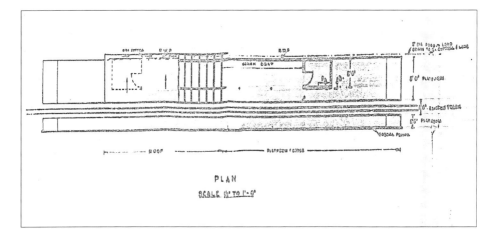

PLAN

SCALE ½" TO 1'-0"

The end elevation is seen here and shows the east platform fence on the left, the gap for the train to pass through, the station building complete with canopy and the grass bank on the right. (Worthing Borough Council)

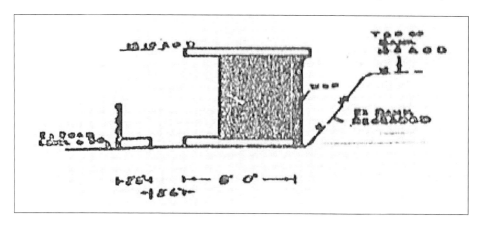

The plan also included a "site plan" showing the location of the proposed station. This can be seen below and shows the word "RED" along with an arrow pointing at the proposed station location. (Worthing Borough Council)

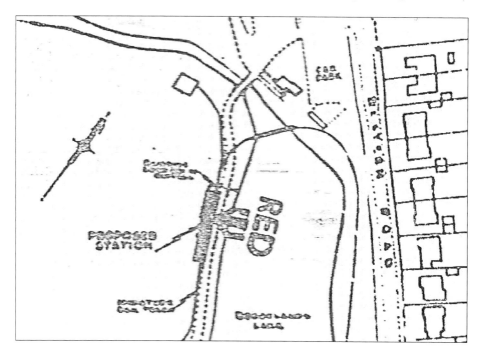

Ernie Woods can be seen below sitting in "Western Comet". Part of the new station can be seen in the background. (Des Weller and Linda Niall)

This photograph, taken in 1969 shows David Stanier sitting in the carriage, while a good friend of his sits in the driving seat of "Western Comet". (Lesley Stanier)

Driver Des Weller is seen here driving "Western Comet" along the east bank.
Note the fuel tank behind "Western Comet's" front windows.
(Des Weller and Linder Niall)

Des Weller on the same day, although on a different journey. The seafront can be seen in the background. (Des Weller and Linder Niall)

In this view Des Weller drives "Western Comet" off the Teville Stream railway bridge. (Doris Walker)

A typical Brooklands Railway shot. Taken in 1973, one can see how quickly the small trees, either side of the track have grown. (Trevor Rowe)

In 1973, the founders, Ernest Woods and David Stanier decided they wanted to retire and sell up. They had both frequented the "Three Horse Shoes" public house in South Street, Lancing for some time now and their plans were mentioned to drinking partner Frank Ransom, better known as Darby. From this conversation, Darby Ransom soon became the owner of the railway and the accompanying attractions.

His wife Shirley soon joined him and during the late 1970's, they decided to spray the class 52 Western locomotive and all six carriages bright red. The windows, front grill and the carriage compartment numbers and lettering were picked out in white, although the loco did retain its white roof and buffers. The hand/grab rails, the builders work plates and the nameplates were picked out in black. Darby and Shirley rather hoped that being more visible, it might attract more visitors to the railway.

Darby Ransom can be seen below sitting in "Western Comet" with Candy, his German Shepherd, while his mother in law's dog stands on the east platform. Note the new ticket office in the background, built to serve all attractions. (Darby and Shirley Ransom)

Not only was the class 52 Western locomotive sprayed red, it was also fitted with a CB radio and aerial to keep in contact with the ticket office. It was also decided that "Western Comet's" seat had become worn and so Darby contacted Severn Lamb Ltd to order a replacement.

Sadly, due to the uniqueness of the loco, Severn Lamb Ltd were unable to help. Many attempts were made to find a suitable seat and in the end a Ford Escort seat was used, although this was much higher than the original, but gave better support for the driver's back.

It is interesting to note that while Darby had ownership of the railway, "Western Comet" had gone through a total of two 1.6 litre Ford Escort engines. I was also interested to learn that in 1976 fares were 12 pence for adults and 8 pence for children.

Three friends of mine await the return of the driver, sometime during the summer of 1985. Interestingly the loco appears to be starting its journey from opposite the boat office. Note the locomotive's windows, which for some reason during the eighties, were clear once again. By 1990 they had been repainted white. (The Ayling Family)

A similar view of the Ayling family. Note the new much higher Ford Escort seat. (The Ayling Family)

"Western Comet" is seen here crossing the bridge on 6th August 1988. By this time wooden cowcatchers had been placed over the wheels of the loco and all six carriages. (Peter Scott)

The Ayling family return for another ride on the miniature railway.
(The Ayling Family)

Another view of their visit showing the café on the left and bungalows
along Western Road in the background. (The Ayling Family)

This photograph, taken during the summer of 1988, shows the train at the south end of the lake, with the pitch and putt course in the background. (Bruce Palmer)

The train prepares to leave the station on 21st May 1989. Note the wooden cowcatchers covering the wheels of "Western Comet". (Antony Everett)

A familiar view of the locomotive coming off the
bridge on 21st May 1989. (Antony Everett)

Darby and Shirley Ransom operated the attractions until 1990, when they too
decided it was time to retire. The railway and other attractions were sold to a
Mr William Hagger. His son Clive joined him the following year and later took
over the ownership of the railway.

Sadly, vandalism at the park had always been a problem and this was
highlighted once again when the station building, which included the booking
office and waiting room, was burnt down. It was decided that the remains of
the wooden structure would be dismantled and not rebuilt.

In September 1992 Clive Hagger purchased an additional loco. This eight-
wheel loco called "Bo Bo", built in 1985 by Mr M. Chapman was purchased
from the Hastings Miniature Railway, which incidentally still runs along
Hastings beach in East Sussex.

While on a trip to Florida, Clive purchased a large aluminium souvenir plaque
showing the name "Dixie" and two American confederate flags. This plaque
was fitted to the front of "Bo Bo" who would then become "Dixie".

One can see from the photograph below that "Dixie" was an unusual looking locomotive. Although powered by a three cylinder Lister diesel engine, it was purposely fitted with a chimney and a boiler (which apparently was an old immersion heater) to give it that steam engine look. (Clive Hagger)

"Western Comet" is seen here on its way along the west bank. Note the fence in the background, which was erected by Southern Water while a major pipe laying scheme was undertaken in the early 1990's. (Clive Hagger)

A 1994 track plan of the Brooklands Miniature Railway can be seen below. The layout shown is exactly the same as it was, when the 10-¼ gauge line opened in 1967. (Peter Scott)

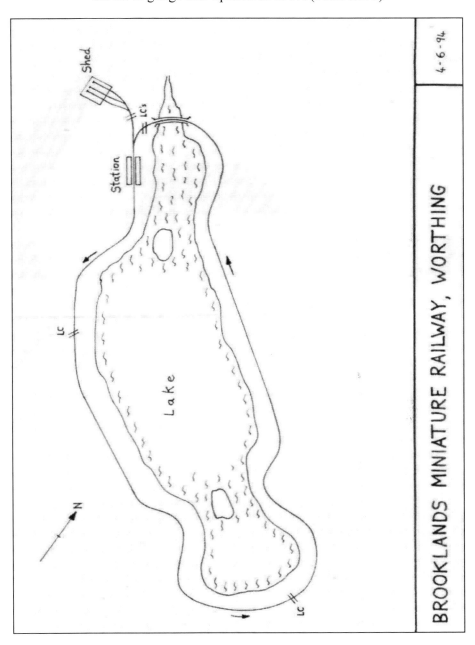

On some occasions Clive found it difficult to staff the ticket office, seen in the background of this photograph. As a result, a sign was fitted to the third carriage explaining; "Please pay on the train, 60p per person". (Clive Hagger)

"Western Comet" is seen here on the west bank and shows the pitch and putt course in the background. Looking at the way the driver is wrapped up suggests that it could have been a rather chilly day! (Clive Hagger)

Clive decided that for added safety all six carriages would have boards fitted to each seating compartment to prevent feet from straying outside the carriages. This is evident in the photograph below. (Clive Hagger)

During the mid 1990's Worthing Borough Council laid a new footpath from the car park by the go-carts, through the pitch and putt course and over the railway to the footpath that follows the edge of the lake. This crossing is seen below and shows the last remaining boat office in the background. The second office was burnt down during the 1970's. (Authors Collection)

One can see from this aerial view, the new pathway leading through the pitch and putt course at the bottom left of the photograph. (Authors Collection)

The photograph below shows the train approaching the boat office. The water level looks particularly low, which could be the reason why the boats are not operating. On busy days "Western Comet" would often stop here to pick up more passengers. (Clive Hagger)

Clive Hagger's father, William, can be seen below sitting in "Western Comet". "Dixie" can just be seen on the left. (Clive Hagger)

A similar photograph is shown below although taken at a different angle. (Clive Hagger)

After much thought Clive decided that "Dixie's" three cylinder Lister diesel engine was far too noisy to give passengers a nice and peaceful train ride around the lake and so the loco was withdrawn from hauling passenger services. The loco was however used as a works unit, which would often be coupled to an open wagon built from scratch by Clive and would both be used for track maintenance or re-ballasting.

The open wagon was built using angle iron for the framework. Once welded together wood was bolted to the base and sides. Clive inquired about purchasing two bogies from a miniature railway builder, however he recalls them being rather expensive.

As the wagon would mainly be used for winter works he decided not to go ahead with the purchase. Instead, when the open wagon was needed, Clive jacked up one of the spare passenger carriages, dropped out the two bogies and put them on the open wagon. This was a simple task and as a result took minutes to perform.

William Hagger can be seen above sitting in the rather claustrophobic cab of "Dixie". In October 1996 "Dixie" was sold to a private owner in North Yorkshire and today survives on a railway in Essex. (Clive Hagger)

In 1998, a local miniature railway enthusiasts group showed an interest in the Brooklands Miniature Railway. Many of its members owned 10 ¼ gauge steam and diesel outline locomotives and it was suggested that Clive Hagger might allow visiting locomotives. Following a conversation with Clive no further action was taken.

A year later, the enthusiasts group made tentative enquiries into the possibility of taking over the Brooklands Miniature Railway. There was however one main concern. The group felt that the curves at Brooklands were too tight and would not only cause extreme wear and tear on their locomotives but could also cause derailment.

Owing to the railway's seaside location, it was noted that the track work was in very poor condition due to the salty air and would require almost complete replacement. With this in mind and the potential cost of purchasing the lease, it was decided to not go any further. The group would later become The South Downs Light Railway Society and can now be found at the Wyvale Garden Centre at Pulborough, West Sussex.

By the time the photograph above had been taken the carriage compartment numbers and lettering had been repainted yellow and "Western Comet's" buffers had been painted black. Two car side mirrors had also been fitted to the side. (Clive Hagger)

A photograph of the engine / carriage shed. Note the two points, splitting the track into three. The boat shed is to be found on the left. This photograph and the following photographs, kindly supplied by Jonathan James, were taken on the 1st July 2001. (Jonathan James)

The Severn Lamb loco sits in the station while fares
are collected by William Hagger. (Jonathan James)

A similar view, although taken from a different angle. (Jonathan James)

The loco is seen here following the path on the west side of the lake.
(Jonathan James)

Continuing south, the train approaches the boat office and landing stage.
(Jonathan James)

"Western Comet" passes over the bridge. Note the ugly looking wing mirrors.
(Jonathan James)

The train slowly pulls into the station. Note the sign on the rear carriage which states; "Train fare 80p or 1 token per person. Under 2's ride free, under 7's to ride with an adult. For your safety keep clear of train at all times. Thank you." (Jonathan James)

Clive Hagger can be seen below driving "Western Comet" around the curve before the Teville Stream railway bridge. In 2001, the mud and grass in the foreground made way for a new tarmac path and crossing, making it easier and safer for visitors to cross the railway. (Clive Hagger)

The new crossing can be seen below with the Teville Stream railway bridge on the left and the café on the right. Fencing and safety signage was also added at the same time. (Authors Collection)

On the hole Clive found "Western Comet" to be a very reliable locomotive. There were the occasional problems with the engine, but that was inevitable. Clive decided to keep a couple of reconditioned Ford engines in the engine shed, which would be swapped out and reconditioned when necessary.

This meant "Western Comet" would only be out of service for as long as it took to take out and refit one of the other engines. Having engineering companies on the nearby Lancing Industrial Estate was also of use on many occasions, especially when Clive needed hydraulic parts or bearings.

It seems as though the car mirrors on the sides of "Western Comet" only survived a short period of time. The drivers soon realised that it was easier to sit on one side of the loco, which meant that they were able to keep a watchful eye on the passengers, instead of peering into two small mirrors.

Sitting on the side also gave the drivers more room to move their legs although the thought of giving up a sprung seat makes me wonder if they ached at the end of the day. I can only presume that the springs on "Western Comet" were first class!

In this view, "Western Comet" is almost visible as it approaches the bank with the retained wall, on the east side of the lake. (Clive Hagger)

The photograph below shows the train in almost the same position, although the photograph has been taken from the other side of the lake and shows the houses alongside Western Road. (Clive Hagger)

By the time this photograph had been taken on 19th June 2002, "Western Comet" had been given a yellow roof and fares had been increased to £1.00 per person. (Peter Lea)

"Western Comet" is seen here on the exact same journey and will shortly pull into the station. (Peter Lea)

The front of the class 52 Western loco is seen here on the same day and shows much of the cab detail, including the works plate. (Peter Lea)

"Western Comet" is seen here just leaving the Teville Stream bridge and is about to pass over the crossing before entering the station. (Clive Hagger)

The photograph below, taken on 20th July 2003 shows the train heading south along the west bank. (Authors Collection)

A view of the lake, looking north, taken from the last carriage on 20th July 2003. (Authors Collection)

Another photograph, taken on same journey, can be seen below and shows "Western Comet" nearing the retained wall. (Authors Collection)

"Western Comet's" cab is seen below. The dials shown on the wooden dashboard include oil temp, water temp, battery amp meter, fuel gauge and speedometer. The large round hole in the center is where a clock would have been, although it is unclear when this was removed. Also to be seen on the dashboard is the knob for the choke and two buttons, one of these being for the horn and the other for the electric ignition.

Below the dash, one can see the throttle and a fuse box on the left, the hydraulic control knob, the gear stick and the gearbox. The handbrake is out of sight on the right of the cab. Note also the rather worn seat and the screw on the top panel, which once unscrewed makes the top panel completely removable. (Authors Collection)

"Western Comet" can be seen below sitting in the station on 13th May 2005, with passengers behind preparing to alight the train. (Authors Collection)

Clive Hagger operated the attractions at Brooklands until early 2006 when he decided that he would focus on his other Worthing attraction, "Peter Pans Playground". The Brooklands Pleasure Park attractions were then sold to a Mr Kevin McCluskey. This new ownership would mean many changes for the park, which would become "DiddlyLand". Mr McCluskey, "The Diddlys" creator had already secured a four-part book deal, aimed at three to eight year olds, as well as developing a 3D animated series narrated by Bernard Cribbins.

"Diddly Dum", a train boy and "Diddly Dee", a train girl, and cheerful Charlie the Station Master all undertake international rescue missions from their home in Tootsville. "The Diddlys" railway attraction comes as Mr McCluskey plans a 26 episode series penned by Tweenies writer Gordon Volke, for children's television.

Not only has Mr McCluskey secured a two-year contract with Harry Ramsdon's to put "The Diddlys" on its children's menu, but it is also being used as the face of the National Railway Safety Campaign throughout schools in the UK.

In the Worthing Herald and Gazette dated Thursday 19th January 2006 and titled "The next Diddly train at platform one will be…" they explained; "Kevin McCluskey plans to transform the East Worthing lake and mini railway into the home of Diddly Dum and Diddly Dee.

Kevin, 44, will submit his final plans to Worthing Borough Council by the end of the week with the hope of opening in February. He hopes his relationship with Worthing Borough Council will be better than the one, which has just ended, with Arun District Council, which owns Hotham Park in Bognor Regis. Kevin ran a successful Diddlys' train at the park for 18 months but, after rejecting the council's terms for a new five-year lease, he was given until Sunday to remove all trace of the Diddlys' train and its Tootsville Station.

Arun wanted Kevin and his business partner, Lynne Carr, to pay £6,000 up front, £1,000 annually, as well as 10 per cent of their gross takings and be subject to business rates. Kevin has accused the council of running him out of Bognor because the railway is "not viable on the amounts they are asking us to pay". But he says he can now focus on Worthing. "There is always good that comes out of bad," he said. "By working in Bognor, I found out about Worthing and the potential here is 10 times better. The councillors here are active and have made suggestions. I am so excited."

The Herald continued to explain; "Kevin, who plans to move to Worthing from Stratford-upon-Avon, aims to invest between £500,000 and £750,000 over the next three years to make Diddlyland a "must" visitor attraction on the Sussex coast. The lakeside train will run all year round, instead of summer only and the boats will be re launched with a pirate theme. A crazy golf course is also planned and will be created out of the old bandstand. In the summer, Kevin also hopes to open the paddling pool, which will be free. He was given permission to open the existing lakeside train and a Santa's grotto for a week before Christmas and attracted 3,200 people."

The complete Hotham Park railway, which included the track, locomotive and carriages were transported to Brooklands. The Hotham Park track was sold and the carriages were dismantled due to them being in a very poor state. The frames and bogies however were kept with the possibility of using them in the future. It was also decided that the Brooklands class 52 Western locomotive was severely worn out and in need of a complete restoration program. Mr McCluskey put "Western Comet" up for sale and within days was purchased for £9.000 by Joe Nemeth of the Berkeley Light Railway in Gloucestershire.

The photograph below shows "Western Comet" on the back of the Berkeley Light Railway's truck. Joe Nemeth's son can be seen preparing to strap the loco to the truck ready for the journey to Gloucestershire. (Joe Nemeth)

I decided to contact "Western Comets" new owner, Joe Nemeth, and ask him about the locomotive's future. Mr Nemeth explained; "For many years I have longed to own a model of a class 52 Western locomotive, and the one I remember well was the "Exmoor Enterprise", which used to run at Minehead. As a small boy I remember many enjoyable trips behind this engine. Sadly the railway is now long gone and the locomotive and stock is in private hands. I always hoped that one day I might find another example and then, at the beginning of 2006 I was fortunate to acquire the one from Brooklands.

We brought "Western Comet" to a new railway, which was opened by Bob Symes of BBC's Tomorrows World in April 2005. It is set out in the spacious grounds of the Cattle Country Adventure Park here in Gloucestershire. The park is located about a mile from the famous Berkeley Castle and the old Sharpness Docks on the banks of the River Severn and is within 30 minutes from either Bristol or Gloucester. The Brooklands locomotive is in a poor state having worked hard for nearly 40 years. She has lost much of her original detail, but will undergo a full rebuild where she will be restored to her original specification, and may be in action for our September 2006 gala."

Now "Western Comet" had gone the brightly coloured, red, yellow and blue locomotive from Hotham Park named "Diddly Dum" would now be coupled to the original Brooklands carriages and would be responsible for taking visitors on a pleasant trip around the lake.

Kevin McCluskey can be seen above with Brooklands new locomotive "Diddly Dum". The photograph, taken near the boat office and landing stage, was taken in April 2006 by the Worthing Argus to advertise the Easter train rides. For some reason, the original Brooklands toast rack style carriages have not been included in this shot.
(The Argus / Newsquest Ltd)

"Diddly Dum" itself is in fact completely powerless. The fibreglass shell, which resembles a steam engine, sits on a modified Hotham Park carriage frame and uses the original bogies. The tender behind "Diddly Dum" is the power unit, which encases a 1700 diesel engine, however it is driven using the controls in "Diddly Dum". This eight-wheel powered unit was originally a diesel outline loco and built by a Mr J. Hurdell in 1985. It was modified by Kevin McCluskey before coming to Brooklands, however still retains the original framework within.

A closer view of the tender power unit can be seen below. (Authors Collection)

The tender bodywork was built in such a way, so it could be lifted off with ease to gain access to the engine. The power unit is seen here in July 2006 without the tender bodywork and shows the original locomotive framework. (Authors Collection)

"Diddly Dum" sits in the shade, having just been brought out of the shed and is being made ready for a hard day's work. (Authors Collection)

Once ready "Diddly Dum" is driven the short distance to the station where it sits and awaits its first load of passengers. "Diddly Dum" is slightly wider than "Western Comet" and so as a result, the concrete platform had to be altered to accommodate him. (Authors Collection)

A 2006 track plan of the Brooklands Miniature Railway can be seen below. Although the 10 ¼ gauge track layout has remained the same throughout the course of history, this plan shows the additional level crossings which were added during the mid 1990's and in 2001 (Peter Scott)

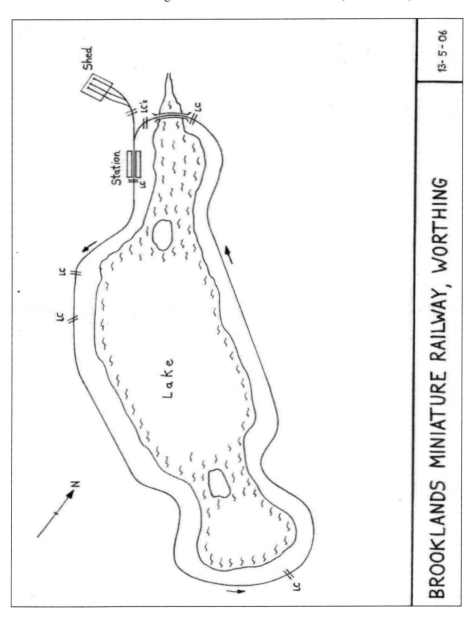

"Diddly Dum" is seen once again, this time with a few passengers on board. The train is heading south along the west bank of the lake having just past the boat office and landing stage. (Peter Scott)

"Diddly Dum's" journey is almost over as he passes over the Teville Stream railway bridge. (Peter Scott)

Shortly after Kevin arrived at Brooklands, plans were designed to modify the original Brooklands carriages into enclosed carriages and in June 2006 work began to construct the wooden sides, ends and roof for each carriage. Whilst visiting the railway to look at this new project, I found the remains of Clive Hagger's open wagon. Due to it's condition, the wagon was later disposed of.

One of the newly constructed wooden coach sides and one
coach end can be seen below. (Authors Collection)

Work also began in June to build the second locomotive, "Diddly Dee". This loco was also designed as a dummy loco and the fibreglass shell, built by Kevin McCluskey, would also be lowered onto another modified Hotham Park carriage frame and would retain the existing carriage bogies.

Since the new Severn Lamb stock was delivered in 1967, generally only three out of the six carriages were ever used. The idea was that "Diddly Dum" would remain at the front with the tender, while pulling three carriages, and "Diddly Dee" would be coupled to the last carriage and the spare three carriages would then be coupled behind. Children would be allowed to sit in "Diddly Dee" making them believe that they are the driver for the last three carriages.

The photograph below shows the shell of "Diddly Dee"
being built out of fibreglass. (Authors Collection)

Kevin McCluskey can be seen below working on "Diddly Dee's" face.
(Authors Collection)

An advert which appeared in many local newspapers throughout summer 2006.
(The Argus and Sentinel)

The enclosed carriage project continued. The idea would be that when all the sides, ends and roof for each carriage had been built, the existing carriage sides would be taken away from the frame and stored. The enclosed carriage bodywork would then be bolted to the original Brooklands framework and would retain the original bogies.

Kevin admitted that the Severn Lamb Ltd "toast rack" carriages were getting rather tatty. Over the years the red paint had faded and had become worn and chipped in many places. As a result, these areas had revealed the original blue livery. Due to this, Kevin wanted to press on with the enclosed carriage project. Meanwhile Kevin had contemplated rubbing these original carriages down and re-spray them, however it was decided not to go ahead with this idea.

The photograph above, taken on the 10th July 2006 shows the spare set of carriages being dismantled ready for the new enclosed tops to be added. The builders work plates, carriage numbers and lettering were also removed and stored. (Authors Collection)

An example of the builders work plate can be seen below. Sadly when the carriages were painted in the 1970's the paint clogged up the lettering. As explained earlier the plate reads; "Design by David Curwen – Made by Severn Lamb Ltd – 1967 – Stratford on Avon." (Authors Collection)

An example of BMR lettering can be seen below. (Authors Collection)

An example of the overlapped letters S and W (Stanier and Woods)
can be seen below. (Authors Collection)

An example of a carriage compartment number can also seen.
(Authors Collection)

Shortly after I visited Kevin and his team again to follow up their progress on the railway. I was greeted and told that they had found something I may find of interest. I was pleasantly surprised when I realised it was a painting of "Western Comet". Kevin and his team were having a thorough tidy up when they discovered it at the back of one of their sheds. I was told I was welcome to have this painting, as it was destined for the skip.

I contacted Darby Ransom and asked if he remembered it. He was not so sure, however having taken it with me on a visit to his home, it suddenly brought back memories for both him and his wife Shirley. He explained to me that he had commissioned Alun Powell, a family friend, to sign write various signs within the park.

This painting, measuring 18 x 48 inches, was painted around the same time and was signed in the bottom right hand corner "Alun 1987". Painted on perspex, the painting was then hung on the rear of the ticket office, located near the railway bridge.

Clive Hagger also recalls the painting and explained to me that he fixed it, along with the train timetable to two posts next to the path that led to the trampolines. During this time the painting was damaged by vandals, so Clive riveted a sheet of steel to the back, along with two wooden batons to give it more strength. Clive also recalls that another painting was done showing the locomotive and all the carriages, but sadly today, its whereabouts is unknown.

The painting can be seen above. Note Frank (Darby) Ransom's initials on the work plate below the front side window and the missing engine cover above the side grills. (Authors Collection)

To my surprise, while continuing with my research, a photograph was passed on to me which actually showed this particular painting attached to the timetable / information board. The photograph, taken on 19th June 2002, can be seen below. (Peter Lea)

"Diddly Dum" is seen here on 29th August 2006, heading towards the café. Western Road can be seen on the right of the photograph. (Authors Collection)

In this view shown below, "Diddly Dum" has crossed the Teville Stream railway bridge and is about to enter the station. (Authors Collection)

On 31st August 2006 a major change occurred. Instead of passenger services travelling anticlockwise around the lake, it was decided to change the direction of the journey and take the train round in a clockwise direction. "Diddly Dum" therefore had to be turned round, although there was no need to turn the carriages as a coupling already existed at the end of the three-carriage set.

The reason for changing the direction was mainly down to the large numbers of visitors expected for the Halloween train rides. It was thought that the driver would have a better view of visitors about to cross the crossing by the station, rather than coming off the Teville Stream railway bridge and having the view partially blocked by the ticket office.

It was also thought that by going clockwise, traffic waiting at the traffic lights on the eastbound carriageway of the A259 Brighton coast road, would see the front of the train, rather than the back, causing them to pull into the park for a train ride.

Having mentioned this to Darby Ransom, he expressed his concern and explained that the curve directly outside the north end of the station could cause problems. Darby pointed out that "Western Comet" needed the straight on the south side of the station to gather up speed for its first corner. If the driver needed to stop the train before or on a curve due to a duck, swan or visitor being in the way, "Western Comet" would find it difficult to get going again due to wheel spin, especially in wet or icy conditions.

It was thought that "Diddly Dum" would become the first, on the 10-¼ gauge line, to successfully pull a passenger service in the opposite direction. However a few days later, on a wet and rainy day, the driver of "Diddly Dum" experienced this same problem on the curve just outside the north end of the station. Evidently having problems, the train was pushed at the rear by a colleague, until it picked up traction. The train finished its journey without any other problems but it was decided that the clockwise direction would be scrapped. The locomotive was turned round and services were reintroduced in the original anticlockwise direction.

Having been granted planning permission and in preparation for Halloween, on 7th September 2006 Kevin and his team began work on station improvements. Mechanical equipment had been hired to dig away five feet of the bank on the west side of the station platform. The plan was to enlarge the station platform, which would then be decked with wood.

The station can be seen below looking in a southerly direction. The grass bank on the right would make way for a larger platform. The digger can be seen on the right removing the bank. (Authors Collection)

On Thursday 14th September 2006, the Brooklands Miniature Railway featured in the Worthing Herald. The Herald wrote; "While thousands flocked to Worthing to relax, holiday and enjoy the summer sunshine, a dedicated workforce rolled up their sleeves and prepared for their busiest time of year. Now, as summer draws to a close and the children return to school, reporter Katherine McGlinchey chats to those who were on the front line."

Brooklands Pleasure Park was one of the attractions mentioned. Titled "We had a rail good time", reporter Katherine McGlinchey explained; "Seafront pleasure park Brooklands is in the middle of a revival. This season, it was taken under the wing of Kevin McCluskey, former manager of Hotham Park in Bognor Regis. Despite his short time there, he said his first season at the Brighton Road park had been a success, with as many as 1,000 people showing up on the hottest of days."

Kevin McCluskey explained; "It was great when the weather was warm and sunny, but August was a bit of a disappointment as it was raining most of the time. Overall though, business has been good and many tourists, as well as locals who remember the park from when they were young, have come to enjoy the facilities."

The reporter continued to say; "Since taking over, Kevin has reopened the miniature railway and the continuing rejuvenation will see the boating lake once again taking guests on a serene water tour. He is getting trampolines put in and wants to create an indoor play area themed as a castle. A former builder, Kevin, 44, is very hands on and is building new train carriages and refurbishing the station for the miniature railway himself.

He moved to Sussex from Stratford-upon-Avon almost three years ago with his wife and three children. He said: "I've been doing this sort of job for so long that I barely notice I'm working when everyone else is on holiday. I enjoy it; people are in a happy mood when they come here. They bring their kids to have a good time and its lovely to see."

The photograph above shows the amount of progress that had been made to the station. Platform foundations had been added and wooden decking was in the process of being laid. (Authors Collection)

The photograph below, taken on Sunday 24th September 2006 shows two of the proposed six enclosed carriages. One can see "Diddly Dum" at the front, followed by three original untouched Brooklands carriages, two new enclosed carriages (part finished and painted red and yellow) and the frame of the sixth Brooklands carriage. All enclosed carriages were to be built on the original Severn Lamb Ltd frames. (Authors Collection)

Between Saturday 21st October and Tuesday 31st October 2006 Kevin held "Halloween Fright night". Visitors arriving between 5pm and 8pm could view the northern island, which had been transformed into a haunted atoll, and take a spooky train ride around the lake accompanied by Dracula, Frankenstein, Werewolves, Skeletons, and Witches for just £2.50.

Visitors to the park could also visit a haunted castle with dungeons, torture chamber, a graveyard, and a witches den for only £1.50. The Diddly's café was open during this time, giving visitors the chance to sample some of Dracula's blood or some witches brew.

An advert for the 2006 Halloween event, which appeared in the local newspapers. Similar adverts could be found on site. (The Argus and Sentinel)

Kevin and his team's hard work was not going unnoticed. By now it was evident that many visitors, the local newspapers and Worthing Borough Council had acknowledged and praised the improvements happening at the park. An end of season report compiled by Worthing Borough Council stated the following; "Visitor numbers to Brooklands seem to be sharply increasing with the innovations brought in by the new concessionaire. Theming the park on the Diddly characters and reopening the paddling pool have been major drivers in this."

Photographed on Thursday 30th November 2006, one can see from the photograph that the first two carriages were progressing well.
(Authors Collection)

Between Saturday 9th and Sunday 24th of December 2006 a Christmas event was held. Christmas decorations were added to the station and "Diddly Dum's" tender was made into a sleigh. For just £2.00 visitors were able to take a ride on the train and could look out for Father Christmas, several snowmen and Christmas trees positioned along the route. The visit was not complete without seeing Father Christmas in his grotto before leaving the park.

The photograph below, taken on 17th December 2006, shows "Diddly Dum's" sleigh tender and two finished enclosed carriages. (Authors Collection)

The Christmas event had proved to be very successful indeed with over 13,000 people of all age groups visiting the park between Saturday the 9th and Sunday 24th December 2006. Due to this success and the success of the Easter and Halloween events, Kevin McCluskey was now able to pencil in further events for the future.

There was however one disappointment. Towards the end of the Christmas period and on one journey in particular, it soon became apparent that the two enclosed carriages would be withdrawn from service immediately. This decision came as strong winds, blowing in from the sea, made the two enclosed carriages rather unstable as they approached the south end of the park.

With safety taking priority it was decided that the enclosed carriage project would be scrapped and the existing open carriages be retained. A total of three enclosed carriage tops had been built although only two had been put onto the Severn Lamb frames.

Kevin admitted it would be a shame to destroy these enclosed tops after so much work had been put into building them, so it was decided that they would be taken off their frames, stored and then eventually placed on the station's west platform.

"Diddly Dum" continued service with the untouched three-carriage set, while the spare three-carriage set remained dismantled. Shortly after, the red enclosed carriage top was placed on the west platform along with a topiary privet, in the shape of a steam locomotive. This carriage now provided somewhere for the visitors to sit while they waited for the train.

During March 2007, Kevin began to re-spray the complete three-carriage set. One by one, they were taken out of service, lifted from the track and rolled into the boat shed for preparation. The wooden seats were removed, rubbed down and then re-varnished.

Two of the carriages had their builders work plates, carriage numbers and lettering removed, before being rubbed down and sprayed orange and purple. Summer and the hot weather were on its way and time was not on their side.

As a result of this, the middle carriage was spared of its work plate, carriage numbers and lettering, and was given a quick, blue paint job. This carriage would then be finished properly at a later date.

All three carriages had black padded waterproof cushions added to the seats and the first and last carriage also had the boards, intended to stop feet from straying outside the carriage, lowered.

It was also decided at this time that the carriage numbers, lettering and builders work plates would be disposed of and not used on the carriages. I was fortunate to rescue all of these from the complete third carriage as souvenirs. The blue carriage now remained the only carriage out of the six to retain these.

Easter came round once again, which meant two members of staff would have to wear, just like last year, the Easter chick and bunny costumes. I wonder if they got paid any extra for that? The weather could not have been better and the whole event was once again a success.

In June, the yellow enclosed carriage top had been placed on the west platform to accompany the other and a concrete ramp was constructed to make it easier to gain access onto the west platform. By now "Diddly Dee's" fibreglass shell had been sprayed, although the face still awaited final improvements and a fence with a gate had been erected by the engine/carriage shed. This had now enclosed the works area from general viewing and had also provided better security.

The two enclosed carriage tops with the topiary steam locomotive.
(Authors Collection)

The new fence and gate, which has now enclosed the engine/carriage shed and works area from general viewing. (Authors Collection)

No train's today! On Friday 20th July 2007, the entire country experienced much flooding due to heavy rainfall. Brooklands lake rose to a level which allegedly had never been seen before.

Both photographs show the tracks on the eastern side of the lake partly underwater. (Authors Collection)

Improvements to the park continued and in September 2007 a wooden framework with aluminium sheet roofing was constructed over the track just outside the engine/carriage shed. This would provide additional shelter and storage space.

"Diddly Dum" was also given an additional extra – moving eyes. This was achieved by removing the eyes and inserting new eyeballs to car wiper motors located in the face. I had found this an ingenious idea and realised Kevin's attention to detail.

A CD player was also added to the loco around this time, to play appropriate children's music, such as Disney CD's. Speakers were fitted to the complete three-carriage set and were carefully concealed under the seats.

"Diddly Dum" passes over the site of the original south terminus on Saturday 22nd September 2007. The photograph shows the A259 Brighton coast road on the left and one of a handful of old motor boats carefully positioned alongside the bank of the lake, now used as flower beds. (Authors Collection)

"Diddly Dum" can be seen on the same journey, heading back to the station along the eastern bank of the lake. (Authors Collection)

The 2007 Halloween event took place from 20th – 31st October and like previous years, proved to be very popular. The following month, the third enclosed carriage top was placed on the platform alongside the other two. The Christmas event would follow, taking place between 9th – 24th December.

Over the Christmas period of 2007, a visitor to the park accidentally fell into the lake. Suffering from hypothermia, an ambulance was called. Uncertain of his location, the Brooklands train was commandeered by South East Coast Ambulance Service (NHS) paramedics to quickly locate and then transport the man to the café, where the ambulance was parked.

"Diddly Dum" approaches the boat office and landing stage on Saturday 2nd February 2008. (Authors Collection)

A passenger view of the loco approaching the café and the Teville Stream railway bridge. Note the new dovecot. (Authors Collection)

"Diddly Dum" nears the end of one of its journeys on Saturday 2nd February 2008. The third, white, enclosed carriage top can be seen on the west platform. (Authors Collection)

Come April 2008, fares were still £1.00 per person, the spare set of Severn Lamb carriages remained dismantled and the building of the "dummy" locomotive "Diddly Dee" had been put on the back burner for the time being.

Having spoken to Kevin about his future plans for the railway he explained; "All six carriages will be given open top fibre glass shells complete with doors, "Diddly Dee" will eventually accompany the rolling stock and a station building will be built on the platform alongside the enclosed carriage tops. There is even a possibility we may build a tunnel somewhere along the route. Our Easter, Halloween and Christmas events have been very popular so these will continue to take place."

Overview

Many years have passed since the railway was originally laid in 1965 and after all these years, I am pleased that the railway still exists. I would be interested to know how many visitors have actually travelled on the railway. I'm sure the number would be quite surprising.

I presume there is always a danger that the railway could one day be taken up, for whatever reason, something which would deeply sadden many, including myself. However, the railway is still popular with children and adults alike and it's future, at the moment, seems to be very secure.

I honestly believed that the Brooklands Miniature Railway project would be a fairly simple subject to write about. When I began gathering information I soon realised that it would become more involved than I imagined and surprisingly enough, made the same comment with my previous book projects. I have certainly achieved what I set out to do and have found researching this subject very interesting.

I understand that some of the photographs shown have been repetitious, especially the ones of "Western Comet", although have felt obliged to show them to give a thorough photographic account.

Incidentally "Western Comet" was sold to a Mr Peter Bowers in March 2007 and can now be seen, fully restored at the Royal Victoria Railway in Southampton, Hampshire. "Western Comet" has now been sprayed mid Brunswick green and has been renamed "Western Explorer".

As for the souvenirs rescued from the Brooklands Miniature Railway, which at this moment in time are safely in my possession, it is my intention to pass these on to the Worthing Museum and Art Gallery.

Although this book includes a detailed history of the railway, I will continue to collect any other information, postcards or photographs and will also continue to record any changes that may happen to the railway in the future, with the possibility of compiling further editions. As a result of this, I welcome any comments or additions.

Graham Lelliott

Acknowledgements

My sincere thanks go to the following people and sources used especially those who have kindly given permission to use photographs;

Tim Yates
Geoff Gourd
Mike Franklin
Darby Ransom
Shirley Ransom
Clive Hagger
Kevin McCluskey
Neville R. Knight
Doris Walker
Alun Powell
Peter Scott
Derek Smith
Martin Hayes
Joe Nemeth
Peter Bowers
Chris English
Colin Evans
Roy Larner
David Holroyde
Bruce Palmer
Bill Gage
Chris Taylor
Malcolm Stride
Katherine McGlinchey
Cliff Harrison
Trevor Rowe
Peter Lea
Jonathan James
Therese Williams
Lesley Stanier
Des Weller
Linda Niall
Antony Everett
Nick Kelly
Peter Bryant

The Ayling Family
Jan Simms
The late Wilfred Simms
Worthing Borough Council
Worthing Library
Worthing Museum and Art Gallery
Worthing Herald and Gazette
Worthing Homes Ltd
Portsmouth Publishing and Printing Ltd, West Sussex Division
The Argus and Sentinel
Newsquest (Sussex) Ltd
The West Sussex Gazette
The West Sussex Records Office, Chichester, West Sussex
Model Engineers Magazine / Encanta Media, Orpington, Kent
Miniature Railway Magazine / A to B Magazines, Dorchester, Dorset
Severn Lamb Ltd, Stratford upon Avon
Joe Nemeth Engineering Ltd
Postcard Cabin, Worthing, West Sussex
Constance Postcards Ltd, Littlehampton, West Sussex
The Narrow Gauge Railway Society
The 10 ¼ Society
Miniature Railway World
Miniature Railway World Forum
UK Miniature Railways
Rail Romances, Chester, Cheshire
The Berkeley Light Railway, Gloucestershire
The Royal Victoria Railway, Southampton, Hampshire
The South Downs Light Railway, Pulborough, West Sussex
The Littlehampton Miniature Railway, West Sussex
The Hastings Miniature Railway, East Sussex

I would also like to thank the following for kindly publishing my Brooklands
Miniature Railway inquires in order to help me further this project;

Worthing Herald and Gazette. Article published in December 2006.

Miniature Railway Magazine. Articles published in issue 4/Spring 2007.

Freelance Market News. Article published in issue 2/September 2007.